PERSONAL BANKING

This No Nonsense Guide explains:

★ How banks work and how to choose the best one for you

★ The different types of checking accounts available today

★ Savings and investment accounts

★ Common types of bank loans

★ Other services banks offer

THE NO NONSENSE LIBRARY

NO NONSENSE FINANCIAL GUIDES

OTHER NO NONSENSE GUIDES

NO NONSENSE FINANCIAL GUIDE ®

PERSONAL BANKING

Edward Lehwald
Christine Hanley

Longmeadow Press

PERSONAL BANKING

Copyright © 1990 by Bookman Publishing,
an Imprint of Bookman Dan!, Inc., Baltimore, MD

No Nonsense Financial Guide is a trademark controlled by
Longmeadow Press.

ISBN 0-681-40972-X

Printed in the United States of America

0 9 8 7 6 5 4 3 2 1

PREPARED FOR LONGMEADOW PRESS BY BOOKMAN PUBLISHING

MANAGING EDITOR: John D. Peige

CREATIVE DIRECTOR: Judy Craven-Madison

COVER ART: Melissa Nalewaik

COPY EDITOR: Elena Serocki

PROOFREADERS : Karen Dixon, Anna Maria Eades

CONTENTS

1. HOW DO BANKS WORK?

When most of us use the term "banks," we include savings and loans (S&Ls) and even credit unions. All compete for your dollars and it is your dollars that make them profitable. As you understand where the bank gets its income, you will be in a better position to understand where you have leverage and why one bank may be more responsive to your account than another.

Bank Income

Banks get income from only two sources: money they earn by lending your account balance to others and from fees paid to them for services. This income is generated from deposits and fees of individuals as well as deposits and fees from corporate customers.

Interest Income

Money is a commodity, and its price is its interest rate. Banks buy and sell money, trying to buy it at low interest rates and sell it at high ones. The bank "buys" the use of your money by paying interest on your account. It "sells" the use of your money at a higher interest rate to borrowers. This "spread," or difference between the amount of interest paid on your account and the amount of interest the borrowers must pay, is how the bank makes most of its money. The bank uses its spread to pay its expenses, and whatever money is left over becomes the bank's profits.

It's not just your local bankers huddled in the board room cackling over how they can manipulate interest rates and trying to get something for nothing that determines how interest rates are set, however. The United States Treasury and the Federal Reserve have something to say about it.

While your bank is, on the surface, basically free to pay and charge whatever it wants for interest, the overall level of interest rates is determined by officials in the government. For many years, the government considered it to be good public policy to ensure that banks made profits. This was believed to be a way to ensure the safety of your money and the soundness of the financial system. If you owned a bank and were not a crook, government regulation practically guaranteed that you couldn't go broke.

The trade-off banks made for that virtual guarantee of profitability was that the amount of that profitability was limited. Banks could only make so much money—and no more. That is why, for many years, bank stocks were not much in demand among sophisticated investors.

The consumer's trade-off was that the government limited the amount of interest that the bank could pay for your deposits and, to a lesser extent, the amount of interest the bank could charge you for your loans. A benefit to you was that banks still wanted to compete for your deposits. Since they couldn't compete on interest rates, they competed for your business with "free" services or with "gift" items such as blankets and clocks.

With deregulation, that has all changed and is continuing to change. Now banks are free to pay whatever they wish on deposits (other than business checking accounts) and much freer to charge what they wish on loans. They are also allowed to make different kinds of loans and, in some cases, actually move into other businesses, such as discount stock brokerage operations and insurance.

Banks are much more competitive now than they ever have been. So, your money is even more valuable a commodity than before, because it is tougher to get. It also means that you will have many more options from which to pick.

2. THE DIFFERENT TYPES OF BANKS

Countries such as Canada, Switzerland, France, or Japan have only a handful of banking institutions per country. In sharp contrast, the number of financial institutions offering banking services in the United States is astounding. For example, there are over 37,000 organizations in the United States which call themselves a "bank." Let's take a look at the various categories:

Commercial Banks

There are over 14,000 commercial banks in the United States with over $1 trillion in total assets. They control the bulk of the nation's dollars. The commercial banks tend to be the largest banks in your community.

Their primary services for consumers are loans and checking accounts. Commercial banks do, however, offer the greatest array of services for individuals and are insured by the Federal Deposit Insurance Corporation (FDIC), an agency of the federal government, for up to $100,000 for each individual's total deposits.

Savings Banks

Located primarily in the northeast, savings banks were originally founded to provide loans for building homes. Savings banks are frequently referred to as "mutual" savings banks—mutually owned by the actual depositors, instead of by shareholders. Over 400 exist in the United States today. Savings banks are also insured by the FDIC for up to $100,000 per account.

Savings and Loan Associations

S&Ls, as savings and loan associations are commonly known, range from tiny organizations to those holding billions of dollars. Originally, S&Ls were designed as building and loan associations with membership involving a pooling of money so that members could build their homes. Today there are still building and loan associations in existence and, coupled with the S&Ls, make for over 4,600 in existence nationally. Their total assets are over $629 billion. S&Ls are still the largest lenders of home mortgages and have always had greater branching privileges—the legal ability to establish branch banks, both in and out of state—than commercial banks.

Historically, the insurance covering S&Ls was state chartered and then, later, covered by the federal government in a special fund known as the Federal Savings and Loan Insurance Corporation (FSLIC). As recent events have shown, FSLIC was totally incapable of adequately monitoring and regulating S&Ls in the era of deregulation. The $100 billion "bail out" of these FSLIC insured institutions will haunt taxpayers into the 1990s. The good news is that the federal government is backing the FSLIC guarantee and all depositors will be covered.

Credit Unions

Over 22,000 credit unions exist in the United States, with assets totalling $66 billion. Typically, credit unions were organized by members or employees of a certain company, religious order, or fraternal order for the purpose of providing a limited number of financial services to those participating.

Until recently, credit unions provided such limited services as savings accounts and share drafts (checking accounts) for their customers. Since the Monetary Control Act of 1980, credit unions can offer their customers credit cards, NOW accounts and mortgage loans. The insurance coverage for customers of credit unions is through the National Credit Union Association (NCUA), a federal government agency. Like the FDIC and the FSLIC, the NCUA also insures its deposits to $100,000 per account.

Credit unions are able to offer higher interest rates on deposits and lower rates on loans than commercial banks. This is because their operating expenses are usually lower due to free or low rent on-site facilities (at the sponsoring company or organization). Credit unions also enjoy a tax exempt status on their income, which also lowers their operating expenses.

Thrifts
Mutual savings banks and S&Ls are frequently lumped together and called thrifts.

Bank Holding Companies
A bank holding company is, by law, an organization that holds a controlling interest in the stock of one or more banks. This allows the holding company to engage in profitable businesses outside the traditional banking field, something regular banks are often not permitted to do by banking law.

The Right Bank for a Young Consumer

You know, of course, that you're young, bright, attractive and, with your next raise, are going to join the BMW set just as soon as your boss recognizes these compelling qualities in you . . . probably next week.

The banker knows that you're young and starting out. Not much money. Not much job history. Not the most attractive customer for a bank.

The young consumer usually needs access to credit more than anything else and the bank's willingness to give you credit should be a driving concern when picking a bank account. From a practical perspective, when you don't have much money to save or invest, all banks offer basically similar checking account features.

After you've evaluated the physical convenience of the bank, decide on a checking account based on it's lending policies. Ask the banker some hard questions:

1. Are loans approved by the branch manager or are they approved by a "loan committee?"

2. What are the key elements that the bank uses to make loan approvals?

  • Length of employment?
  • Income?
  • Prior credit history?

If loans can be approved by the branch manager, you will have somewhat more flexibility in negotiating a loan than if the loan is approved by a faceless "loan committee." While the manager has to abide by the credit policies of the bank, (s) he will have more leeway in making an approval based on your "character" than the "loan committee" will. We'll talk more about these elements in Chapter 9.

The Right Bank for Older Consumers

As you get older, and have established your credit worthiness, you should be meeting bankers who can help your savings and investments grow. This is a time when smart shopping can really pay off. You want a banker who will alert you when the bank has special offers or products that will earn you higher interest.

Remember, always, the ultimate responsibility for managing your money is yours. No matter how well intentioned he or she may be, the banker always knows that every time (s)he tells you about an opportunity to earn more than you're earning now, (s)he's costing the bank money. Good bankers will do this anyway on the assumption that by alerting you to these opportunities you will bring them more deposits over the long run. Other bankers only look at the short run increase in their cost and will tell you about opportunities grudgingly, if at all.

Finding the "good" kind is not hard but it requires making an effort to know the people in the branch and making sure that they know you. Building this personal rapport is good but you should also work with the banker to make sure (s)he works on your behalf. A good way to do this is to take competing ads for products or rates that look good to your bank and find out what your bank has that's comparable.

3. HOW DO YOU CHOOSE A BANK?

There are many things that you can, and should, consider when choosing a bank.

There is a strongly held feeling among many people that "all banks are the same," and, like many old sayings, there is much truth in it. So much so that, for most of us, choosing a bank can be based on the answer to one simple question, "Which one is the most convenient for me?" Once you answer that question, a simple comparison between your choices should give you a quick and easy decision.

When you consider all the various factors such as location, and hours of operation which are personally important in determining a bank's convenience, there are some key questions you should ask:

1. First and foremost, you should look at its physical location. Is it easy to drive or walk to, and does it have adequate parking? Is it located on a route to and from work or where you regularly shop?

2. What are the bank's hours? Does it have evening or weekend hours that are convenient for your schedule?

3. Does it have a drive-up teller window? What are the hours of the drive-up teller?

4. Does it have ATMs located on premises with good lighting and safe access after dark?

These are questions you can answer without ever talking to a banker. Once you have determined the answer to these questions, it's time to start looking more specifically at the products the bank has to offer.

Consider Your Situation
What services do you need from a bank? Will this be your first banking relationship, or is it perhaps your last? It is usually during a young person's career that he or she most needs a bank. Later on, the roles are reversed. In the middle and at end of that person's career, the bank usually needs that person more than he or she needs the bank! Early on, a young person may not qualify for loans and may have difficulty finding a banker to work with him. Once the individual has begun to build some assets, then bankers are anxious to be of service. It is reminiscent of the old saw about banks only wanting to lend money to people who don't need money.

Meeting a Banker
Establishing a good banking relationship can, indeed, be difficult—especially for young people just starting out. The best way to get started is to ask someone—from your firm, your family, or a friend—with an established banking relationship to introduce you to his or her banker. If you have no such contacts, then you have no choice but to make your own introduction. In any case, be candid and do not hide any financial information from your banker. Bankers usually have access to this

information through credit bureaus and the like, anyway. Your honesty will help build a mutually respectful relationship which will become invaluable in the future.

Just as you need to realize which banking functions are most important to you, it is equally important to realize that some banks perform certain financial transactions better than others. Your initial contacts with banks should be mutual. That is, you know the banker will be judging you and you should be doing the same to him. Not every bank is right for every person. The results of your work in asking questions of yourself and of various banks will pay off greatly in the end.

When you are choosing between banks, you may think about "good" and "bad" banks. To an extent it is true that, like children, there is no such thing as a "bad" bank. But there may be banks that you should avoid because they are going to be unable to meet your needs. Likewise, there also should be "good" banks that meet your needs and expectations. It is up to you to find out which is which.

You want to find a bank that will give consideration to the amount of business you intend to do with it. If your bank charges full-service fees on your checking account even though you maintain a respectable savings balance there, that may be a poor situation to be in. If you have loans and balances at a bank, and maintain your primary banking relationship there but are charged full service fees on all or most of your accounts, you might want to consider moving your banking relationship elsewhere.

A bank to avoid is one that is slow to clear checks, does not pay interest until that check clears, and

imposes large penalties for early redemption of certificates of deposit. Such penalties, you should know, are no longer required by the federal authorities.

Is your prospective bank convenient? Does it provide high quality, efficient service? How does it compute its interest rates? Does it pay interest on the entire balance—not just the amount above the minimum balance? Answers to these questions will help you find the right bank for you.

4. HOW TO OPERATE A CHECKING ACCOUNT

Checking accounts provide a safe and convenient way to handle your money. You receive a record of your spending, and, if you manage your account wisely, you will build a banking relationship that will help you receive credit when you need it.

How to Write a Check

Writing checks is easy as long as you remember to write clearly—in ink—the date and the amount of the check (in both numbers and words, making sure the two match). Be sure to keep a record of each written check so you can balance your account at the end of the month when your statement arrives.

A common error can occur when you sign your name on the check. The signature that appears on the check should be the same as the one you signed on your signature card at the bank. Another common error is forgetting to sign the check in the first place. If you make a mistake when writing a check, start over. An altered check of any sort looks suspicious and can result in your check not being honored by the bank.

Your checks are your property. Treat them like money. Do not use anyone else's checks or let them use yours, unless you have a joint account with them and their name appears on the check, too.

Endorsing Checks

Endorsing checks is simple and must be done whenever you want to cash or deposit a check made payable to you (such as a paycheck). All it requires is your signature on the back, lefthand edge of the check. You should sign your name exactly as it appears on the front of the check, even if it is misspelled. In such an event, you may then write your correct name underneath the misspelled one.

There are three ways to endorse a check:

1. Write your name only. Do it this way when you are cashing a check. But be careful; once endorsed this way, the check becomes negotiable by anyone. So, if you lose it after you endorse it, you could be out of luck.

2. Write your name with the words "For deposit only" underneath. Do it this way when depositing a check.

3. When you wish to sign the check over to someone else, write "Pay to the order of" the person's name and sign your name underneath. The designated person must then endorse the check, too, when depositing it.

How to Deposit a Check

For your own record keeping, cash or deposit all checks promptly. Banks usually allow about a six month leeway before they refuse to cash "out-of-date" checks, but it can be a real inconvenience to those who wrote the checks. Also, there is always the chance that you will lose a check over time and not even realize it.

Depositing checks requires deposit slips, which normally come from the bank with your supply of checks.

Just fill in the date and the amount to be deposited, and enclose the slip with your deposit. Cash can also be deposited with these slips by filling out the corresponding "cash" line on the slip.

Delays Due to Check Clearing

When your banker talks about waiting for a check to "clear," he means you cannot have access to the money represented by a check you deposit until your bank is paid by the bank where the check originated. This process creates the wonderful world of "float," a process that is an important part of bank earnings and a source of potentially enormous frustration for you.

Float created by the clearing process has two elements: the time it physically takes the check to get from your bank to the other bank (i.e., to be "collected"), and the time it takes your bank to have the money represented by the check made "available" to it. "Collection" float and "availability" float have different impacts.

If your bank puts a "collection" hold on your check when you deposit it, the bank should be telling you that it will take "x" days to physically pay the check and collect the funds from the other bank. If your bank establishes its collection policy in good faith, it is saying that "x" days is the amount of time it will take based on the bank's experience and the efficiency of the Federal Reserve System in processing the item.

A flaw in the system created the opportunity for some banks to profit at the customer's expense. This flaw was created by the process of "availability float." This gets a bit technical, but it's worth walking through to understand why it happens.

Basically, the Federal Reserve (or "Fed"as it is commonly known in the banking industry) establishes standards for the amount of time it takes a check deposited in, say, Philadelphia to be processed through the Federal Reserve System and delivered to the bank in, say, Salt Lake City where it was drawn. These standards do not necessarily reflect the amount of time it actually takes to process the item, but rather the amount of time that it should take.

Not only does the Fed establish a standard processing time, it also gives your bank its money in no more than three days, whether or not the check has actually been processed. If it's not processed, then a new category of float is created called "Fed float," and the government, in effect, lends your bank the money until the Fed collects it from the other bank.

Therefore, when you deposit a $100 check drawn on the bank in Salt Lake City in your bank in Philadelphia, your bank will place a "collection" hold on the check and send it to the Fed for processing. Three days later the Fed gives your bank $100. But, let's say there was a snowstorm in Kansas City and the Fed's plane is grounded for three days. Now it will take six days for that check to physically get from Philadelphia to Salt Lake City. Your bank was paid $100 from the Fed after three days and what did you get? Zilch. You had to wait six days for the money. Your bank got the use of the $100 for free while you were waiting for your money.

To control this process more favorably for you, the Expedited Funds Availability Act (EFAA) became effective September 1, 1988, and forced all banks to adopt standards for check clearing times. The EFAA has curbed some of the more blatant abuses that existed in the old system. Still, there is room for small differences in determining clearing times between institutions, so you should pay attention to this when starting an account. You won't have to ask about it because your bank is required to disclose its policies at the time when you open the account.

What to Do When You Lose Your Checks

In the event that you lose your checks, notify your bank immediately. Incorrect signatures are not always detected, and the bank might process your checks for payment to a thief or other unauthorized persons.

As a practical matter, once you report your checks stolen, the bank will probably want you to close your account and open a new one. The reason for this is that very few banks today actually verify that the signature on a check is yours.

At most banks, and at virtually all large ones, from the time your check is received to the time it is mailed back to you in your statement, it has been handled by machines. Perhaps one check in a thousand will ever be looked at by a human being once it has entered the bank processing system.

It is, therefore, virtually impossible for a bank to detect a forgery on its own. Forgeries are detected once you receive your checks with the statement and report it back to the bank. Once you report it, you will have to fill out a form certifying that the signature is not yours (or— that of any other authorized signer). The bank will then return the money to you and try to collect from the bank where your check was deposited or cashed.

In such an event, you should not have to wait for your money. Your bank is responsible for paying checks only on your signature. If it pays on a fraudulent signature, the bank is stuck for the loss in most cases.

How to Stop Payment on a Check

Occasionally, you may write a check that you do not want paid out. In that event, you can request that your bank place a "stop payment" on it. To do this, you must fill out a stop payment form at the bank. (Most banks will not stop payment by phone.) The bank then has its computer "flag" your account, and personnel are notified not to honor the check.

To accept your stop payment request, the bank will need to know the following information:
- to whom you wrote the check
- the date on which you wrote the check
- the check number
- the check amount

A fee is charged for this service due to the extra effort on the part of the bank. You should be aware, also, that a "stopped" check sometimes gets through the system anyway. A stop payment request is not a legal guarantee and, inevitably, people make mistakes. The bottom line is that the only sure way to keep a check from being cashed is not to write it in the first place. Don't assume you can write a check and change your mind later.

What to Do If a Check Bounces

A check "bounces" when it is not honored by your bank and is returned to the person who cashed or deposited it.

The most common reason for this is a lack of funds in your account. Here are some other common reasons why a check is bounced:

- The check wasn't endorsed properly.

- The person you gave it to held on to it too long before depositing it.

- The funds in your account were not "collected" and a hold was still on them.

Once a check bounces—especially if it is bounced for lack of funds in your account—you will most likely receive a hefty service charge from your bank. You may also receive a charge from the person who deposited your check. Where do all these charges come from and what can you do about them?

First, banks justify their various fees based on the amount of manual processing involved. A check that is "paid" goes through the banking system virtually untouched by human hands. A check that bounces, however, has to be individually looked at, not only at your bank, but at the Fed and any other bank that processed it the first time through. To pay for this extra labor, most banks feel justified in charging as much as $25 or more each time you do it.

Second, the person to whom you gave the check may also charge you a fee if your check is returned. That is because the bank also charges him a fee (usually known as a "returned item" fee) and he feels justified in passing this charge on to you.

Does this sound like banks collect twice for the same bounced check? Well, maybe. If there are two banks involved, one gets the returned item fee and the other gets the bounced check fee. If one bank processes both the returned item and the bounced check, then, yes, the bank does collect twice for the same item.

There is an important message here: Before you open an account, ask about the bank's policies and fees regarding returned items and bounced checks. You will probably find major differences in how much and how often various banks in the same area charge.

You should also find out on what basis will the bank impose the fee. Some banks charge the fee for each check that is bounced. Some charge one fee per day for all checks returned that day. This is obviously an important difference; i.e., if your bank's returned check fee is $20, is it imposed once a day or for each check that clears? All you have to do is be one day late with a critical deposit, and you could easily bounce three or four checks. If your bank charges per check, that could translate into real money with astonishing speed. Clearly, it is in your interest to have a bank that charges *per diem*.

Banks are becoming increasingly sensitive to the issue of these fees. Some banks have even imposed daily limits as to the amount of fees you can run up.

If you do incur these fees, is there anything you can do about them? The answer here is a definite maybe. If you frequently overdraw your account, there is probably nothing you can do or say that will convince the bank to waive any, or all, of the fees.

If, on the other hand, you rarely overdraw your account, you do have a few things to talk about. First,

What Does a Checking Account Cost?

There is a cost, of course, for writing checks—the cost of the checks themselves, for example. You will have a whole range of check styles from which to choose: different color choices, "designer" checks, personalized checks, sports checks, and so on. After you pick the style of check, you will still have to pick the style of the checkbook. There are both wallet styles and book types. The fancier the check, the more the cost will be. For the basic box of 200 checks with your name and address on them, the average cost is usually between $8 and $10.

Learn to Manage Your Checking Account

Just as your bank keeps records of your checking account, you should, too, for sound money management. The bank sends monthly statements, usually processed in "cycles" so that a group of customers all receive statements covering the same group of dates (e.g., June 24-July 24). Another checking account customer at your bank may be on an entirely different cycle. No matter what cycle you are on, however, it will always be the same for you.

The statements are itemized and show all credits and debits of checks or cash. Usually, your cancelled checks are included in the envelope. If you use automated teller machines (ATMs), have your paycheck deposited directly into your account by your company, or have pre-authorized withdrawals from your checking account, these will show up on your statement.

Some banks send out a "profile" statement of your account. Not only do you have a detailed listing of your deposits and credits from your checking account, but

you also have a profile of information about your other accounts at the bank, such as loans and savings accounts. It can be very handy to have all your banking information in one place.

Reconciling Your Statements

Once you receive your banking statement, it is very important to make sure that your records agree with the bank's records. This will ensure that there is no disagreement between you and the bank and, if there is, that any problem can be resolved quickly. To reconcile your checking account, follow these easy steps:

- First, make sure that your checkbook balance is up to date. Subtract any service charges or pre-authorized deductions from this balance to get your most current, "true" checkbook balance.

- Second, sort your checks from within the statement envelope, either by date or by check number. Then match them to the entries you have made in your checkbook register.

- If you come to an entry that doesn't show up on your statement and you don't have a cancelled check, then this check is "outstanding" and has not yet been paid by the bank. List and total such checks on a separate piece of paper, including any outstanding checks from the previous statement.

- Make sure all checks are yours and mark off the corresponding check notation on the statement.

- Make sure that the amount in the credit column matches your deposits. It is important to remember that some of your recent deposits may not yet be included on the statement.

- Subtract the total amount of the checks outstanding from your statement balance.

- Add to this amount any deposits not already included on your statement.

- Incorporate any withdrawals or deposits you have made using an automatic teller machine.

This balance should match your checkbook balance. Most banks print an account reconciliation form on the back of their checking account statements. Use the form or the following one as a guide:

BALANCING YOUR CHECKING ACCOUNT

1. List your checkbook balance   _____
2. Subtract any service charges   _____
3. Your new balance   _____

BANK STATEMENT

1. List your statement balance   _____
2. Subtract any outstanding checks   _____
3. Subtotal   _____
4. Add deposits not credited on statement _____
5. Your checkbook balance should show   _____

How Do Checks Actually Get Cashed?

Each one of your checks may have what looks like a fraction in the upper righthand corner. This "numerator" is the "transit number." This is part of a national numerical system used within the banking industry to identify all banks. The number is in two parts, with a hyphen separating the prefix from the suffix. The prefix uses numbers 1 through 49 to identify cities, 50 through 99 to identify states, and 101 to identify territories and dependencies. The suffix after the hyphen identifies the individual bank in the city, state, or territory.

Directly under the transit number is a "check routing symbol" that is in the "denominator" position. The routing symbol consists of three or four numbers and is assigned only to those banks that participate in the Federal Reserve's check collection system. The number identifies the Federal Reserve facility that should receive the check. It also indicates whether or not the Federal Reserve will give immediate or deferred credit.

Other ways used by banks to help expedite check processing include magnetic ink character recognition (MICR) along the lower edge of each check, which allows checks and any encoded documents to be read directly by data processing equipment. Now all banks have their own system for assigning account numbers to customers with MICR codes pre-encoded on checks and deposit slips. High-speed check sorter readers can handle 1000 or more checks per minute once the information has been encoded.

Every business day, checks accumulate in various bank branches and departments. Checks are then proved and sorted by proof machine operators or MICR sorter

readers. Each check is then endorsed by the bank's stamp to guarantee all previous endorsements and to make the next bank a "holder in due course." Local checks are presented to the next bank by messenger (direct presenting) or through a correspondent bank or local clearinghouse. Members in a clearinghouse maintain settlement accounts with the local Federal Reserve banks or with a correspondent bank instead of settling with one another individually.

Cashing transit or out-of-town checks is far more complicated due to geography and the national policy that a bank may cash or deposit a check that is drawn on a bank thousands of miles away. Transit checks are presented to the bank from which the check was issued through a correspondent bank or the facilities of the Federal Reserve. The twelve Federal Reserve banks serve as centers for check collection in the twelve regions of the country, and ensure that the transit checks flow quickly and efficiently between the regions. These banks pay each other in dollars for the day's transactions and settle net balances through the Federal Reserve headquarters in Washington, D.C. Banks cash these transit checks as a courtesy service to their customers.

For example, a man living in Chicago goes to New York and buys a hat. He writes a check for the hat using his Chicago bank account. The store in New York deposits his check in the store's New York bank. The New York bank forwards the check to the New York Federal Reserve, which in turn sends it to the Chicago Federal Reserve. The Chicago Federal Reserve then returns the check to the Chicago bank where the check was originally drawn to be examined, honored, and charged to the

man's account. The drawee bank then pays the Chicago Federal Reserve for the check. The Chicago Federal Reserve then reimburses the New York Federal Reserve and in turn the hat store receives payment from the New York Federal Reserve.

The Expedited Funds Availability Act (EFAA) will help shorten the time it takes for checks to clear (the float), and the Federal Reserve is charged with the mission of searching for ways to continue to reduce daily float. To speed up the process of clearing checks, the Federal Reserve System has reduced the amount of time for a drawee to decide whether an item should be honored. An experimental electronic information system is currently being tested. Instead of the physical check being sent back to the drawee bank, a magnetic tape with information on all the returned items is sent to the drawee bank. This system of electronic presentment virtually eliminates float. Also, new experimental systems of photocopy transmission—where the image of the check is sent over telephone lines—are other possible ways to eliminate float. However, there is definite customer resistance to alternative receipts for a cancelled or truncated check. Most customers are used to having their actual check returned and do not want a statement or photocopy of the check as their only record.

"Truncating" the service on your checking account is currently offered by quite a few banks. (Banks call it "check safekeeping" instead of check truncation.) Both the Federal Reserve System and the banking industry had hoped there would be more customer acceptance of check truncation, but consumers have not been very receptive. As a society, we are too used to having the

cancelled check serve as a sound legal record for tax and household record-keeping purposes. Banks do record copies of all checks on microfilm, normally charging for a photocopy of the checks. To encourage the use of check truncation services, many banks will offer very low account fees, free checking or other financial inducements. If you're not irrevocably wedded to storing the hundreds of those little pieces of paper that accumulate every year, you might find a bank that offers check truncation. It could save you money!

5. NEW TYPES OF CHECKING ACCOUNTS

Since deregulation, the basic checking account has changed dramatically, both to meet the needs of the American consumer and to keep pace with the increased level of competition among banks. Banks usually refer to checking accounts as "demand deposit accounts" (DDAs) because the money in them can be used by the customer at any time without giving the bank prior notice. There are many different types from which to choose including regular, special, NOW, SUPERNOW, and Lifeline accounts. Why so many different types of accounts today?

Enter Demographics

Today, most banks have segmented their marketplace and identified different groups in their geographical area, separating customers by the size of their account balance(s), and prospective customers by age, income, marital status, etc. Many banks cultivate their high-balance and potential high-balance customers, while discouraging low-balance customers with service charges. How can banks get away with this?

The Effect of Demographics

Typically, banks waive fees and service charges for those accounts that maintain certain minimum balances.

Usually these types of accounts require minimums that are high enough to dissuade the lower balance customers from opening them.

For example, the lower income household that maintains an average balance of $500 per month and writes ten checks (or fewer) each month pays about $92 a year to maintain its account. On the other hand, the average middle-income customer who maintains an average daily balance of $1300 or more and writes twenty-one checks each month pays on average $71 a year to maintain his checking account—$20 less than the lower income consumer.

There is a complete reversal for the more affluent individual who keeps as much as $8000 in his checking account and writes forty or more checks each month. This customer actually earns interest on his account—an average of $260 a year!

Of course, banks aren't usually so crude as to label their accounts by the income level at which they are aimed. Usually they can attract the groups they want by setting "minimum balance" requirements at levels appropriate to various income levels. The higher the income level the bank is trying to attract, the higher the minimum balance needed for "free" service is likely to be. You cannot change your demographic group overnight, but you can minimize any ill effects by shopping for banking services.

Learn to "Shop" for Bank Services

A fair amount of confusion exists over how to select the right checking account, especially since the dramatic changes caused by bank deregulation. As a consumer,

you need to understand that banks are selling services. Just as you would with any good purchasing decision, you need to shop around for the best bank services.

Choosing the wrong checking account can be expensive—perhaps costing you double or triple what it should to maintain that account. When reviewing different checking accounts, do not just look at the fees. Consider other factors like convenient location, a drive-in window, the number of automated teller machines and their locations, and the existence of other services like safe deposit facilities.

CHECKING ACCOUNT CATEGORIES

When you decide to open a checking account, you will have to choose between an individual account, a joint account, and a fiduciary account. All are various types of personal checking accounts, and they are designed for different users.

There is one common requirement among them: all new depositors must sign signature cards. This is necessary to verify signatures on checks and loan forms, to transfer funds, and to give any special instructions to the bank on your behalf.

Individual Accounts

An individual account is for use by only one person, the one who opens the account, signs a signature card, and whose name appears on the check.

Joint Accounts

Two or more depositors may share a single checking or joint account. Typically, husband and wife or parent and

college student have accounts such as this. Legally, both account owners have equal rights to the account.

"Joint tenant accounts" opened with "rights of survivorship" are accounts that, upon the death of one owner, can be claimed by the other owner. This does not mean, however, that claiming the account will eliminate all complications to accessing funds in the account. State laws may govern otherwise, along with provisions in a will, taxes, and general estate proceedings. Of course, you would need to get clarification from an attorney for information in estate cases.

A joint checking account that does not have survivorship privileges is a "tenants-in-common" account. This usually means, both owners must sign all checks and other documents regarding this joint account.

Fiduciary Accounts
Fiduciary accounts are accounts set up as trusts for a minor child or incapacitated adult. An account such as this generally involves a trustee. When children are involved, your bank will probably refer to this as a "Uniform Gift to Minors Account"(UGMA), operated under federal guidelines.

THE FOUR TYPES OF CHECKING ACCOUNTS
There are four basic types of checking accounts: special, regular, NOW, and SUPERNOW. Special and regular checking accounts do not pay interest; the others do.

Special Checking
Special checking typically requires no minimum balance. Instead, a limited number of checks and a monthly

service charge are attached to the account. Some banks provide a small number of checks for "free" with the monthly service charge, and then charge for any checks written above that number. Other banks set a flat fee for all checks written along with the monthly service charge. These special checking accounts are particularly helpful for those with a limited income and strict budget. It allows them to know how much they will pay per month for the account and how much each check they write will cost.

Regular Checking

Regular checking also pays no interest but allows you to offset the monthly service charges by keeping a minimum balance in your account. If the account drops below that level at any given time, your bank will impose service charges for that period of time. Average minimum balances in these accounts tend to be between $350 and $600 a month.

Some of these checking accounts are "tied" to a savings account. Some banks require that the minimum balance be left in the savings portion, while others request it be left in the checking portion. It is important to review all components of your account with your bank when deciding which account to choose.

NOW Accounts

To receive interest on your account, choose the NOW or SUPERNOW account. Typically, both of these accounts have a savings account tied into them. As with regular accounts, the minimum balances can be left in either savings or checking, depending on the bank's policies.

The NOW account generally pays 5-5.5 percent on the account, usually at a fixed rate of interest. The amount of interest you receive may be dependent on the balance level in your account—the greater the balance, the greater the interest. The NOW and SUPERNOW accounts frequently have these "tiered" interest rates, whereby higher interest is paid on higher balances. If your balance drops below your minimum amount, the penalties (in service charges) tend to be considerably greater than those of a regular checking account. On average, minimum balances tend to run between $1000 and $1500.

Some banks are now offering "blended" interest rates, which usually comprise different interest rates at different balance levels, "blending" them to give an average of the different interest rates on the account over a fixed time frame. This produces a lower rate of interest than that of the tiered interest rate, where your entire balance receives the highest interest rate level.

The worst type of interest calculation on an account like this is the "low minimum balance" calculation. This method allows you to earn interest only on the lowest balance on deposit in the account during the entire statement cycle. In other words, if you had $10,000 on deposit for twenty-nine days of a thirty-day cycle, then withdrew it for a major purchase, you would earn no interest for that cycle—and might even be subject to punitive service charges because of your "low" balance. On a tiered basis, your account would be paid interest at the $10,000 level. Quite a difference! On a blended basis, your account would be averaged: $9667. Again, quite a significant difference!

SUPERNOW Accounts

The SUPERNOW account is very similar to the NOW account. Instead of paying a fixed rate of interest, however, a "market" rate of interest is paid, depending on the balance. A few years ago, when interest rates were higher than they are today, these accounts were particularly appealing to high-balance customers. Today, in this environment of lower interest rates, the SUPERNOW account has less appeal. Balance requirements and penalty fees (if the minimum balance is not maintained) tend to be greater than with the NOW accounts.

OTHER SERVICES

Lifeline Checking and Savings Accounts

Under pressure from several consumer-oriented groups, some banks have instituted Lifeline checking and savings accounts. These are low-cost accounts that help to ensure that the elderly and the poor have access to banking services at reasonable rates and are not priced right out of the marketplace. They usually have income and/or age requirements. Since they are completely free, Lifeline accounts generally include only the most basic account services.

"Bundling" Services

While you are evaluating the different types of checking accounts, you may come across a checking account that incorporates many different services. Banks refer to these as "bundling of services" or "package accounts," where everything you might need from a bank is managed under one account.

There is a checking and savings component of this account along with ancillary services such as traveller's checks, stop payment on checks, discount on loans, insurance group rates, and so on. There is usually one monthly fee to cover the many services.

While the packaged account may sound great, be sure that the services in the account are the ones you would be using anyway. If they aren't, you could end up paying more than if you shopped more selectively. The monthly fee for a packaged account can range from $10 to $25 each month, depending on the exact number of specialized services offered.

Free Checking?

Banks sometimes offer to provide you with "free checking" when you open some other account with the bank, such as a savings account, a time deposit account, a money market account, or even a credit card. When looking at a checking account that is tied to an interest-bearing account, be sure that no interest is forsaken and that the interest rates are competitive with those that are being offered by other banks.

Sometimes "free checking" is offered if your mortgage is at that bank and you let the bank automatically deduct the mortgage payment from your account. Again, be sure the mortgage is right for you and that the checking account meets your criteria.

In summary, there are rarely any "free" checking accounts these days. You pay for your checking in one of two ways: by paying monthly service charges and fees, or by maintaining certain balance levels to meet account requirements. By keeping the minimum balance in a

non-interest-bearing-checking account or a low-interest savings account, you may be in a position where you are losing interest income.

A bank lends out specified amounts of money as loans to produce interest income for itself. It can count on those minimum deposits as funds that will stay with the bank as long as the bank keeps the customer satisfied. On interest-bearing accounts, the bank shares some of its profits with you by paying you interest. Just be careful not to incur any fees, as that will make your profits in interest disappear quickly.

Relationship Banking

Lately, banks have been emphasizing "relationship banking" in their promotional materials and, in some cases, their management style. They are trying to "lock in" a customer by creating as many opportunities as possible for the customer to use the bank's services. This will help the bank, of course, but, in many ways, it helps the customer, too—especially if the customer takes the time to get to know the manager or other officers of the bank. There may be times when you need a bank officer's signature on a document or approval for credit. Knowing a banker can be invaluable at such times. Bankers can often waive fees, too.

Money Orders

Sometimes people prefer not to open their own checking accounts, but instead purchase individual blank checks in order to pay their bills and other debts. These are money orders, and they are returned to the bank after each one has been cashed. When you use money orders,

be sure to retain the receipt that came with it at the time of purchase; it will be your only handy proof.

Traveler's Checks

Traveler's checks are particularly helpful when you wish to carry large amounts of cash with you but want a safer way to do so—such as on a trip. They come in several denominations and must be signed in the presence of a bank officer when purchased. To use the checks as cash, you then must sign them in the presence of the person you are paying (the payee, in bank talk). The person cashing the checks can then compare signatures to make sure they are the same.

How Banks Determine Service Charges

The cost of a checking account is determined by the way the bank calculates the balance on that account. Two different ways that banks calculate balances are by assigning a fee to the account if the balance goes below the stated "low minimum balance" at any time during the month (or statement cycle); or if the monthly average of each day's balance (average daily balance) goes below the stated minimum. The key difference between these accounts is that the penalty fee is incurred on any one day during the statement cycle for the low minimum balance account, instead of a monthly average that takes into consideration the natural fluctuations of a checking account. Most banks calculate the balances based on the low minimum balance because it is more profitable to the bank. However, there are still plenty of banks that offer the average daily balance calculations which are more advantageous for you.

There is one other way that a few banks calculate minimum balances. As part of the drive to encourage "relationship banking," banks will total up all deposits at the same bank—including savings and time deposit accounts. They will then use this sum to determine whether it meets the minimum balance calculations. Usually this minimum balance is substantially higher than that of a checking account.

Other Ways of Computing Balances

Other terms you will hear when asking how a bank calculates its minimum balances in checking accounts is "available balance" and "ledger balance." The "balance" on your account refers to the status, or amount of money, in your account. It is important to ask your bank which type of balance calculation it uses to manage the funds in your checking account and over what period of time (daily versus monthly), especially when calculating minimum balances for service charges.

Ledger Balance

A ledger balance is the amount on deposit that shows on the bank's book during any given day. This balance may include a substantial amount of float, as deposited items are given immediate credit in your account, even if the checks have not cleared.

Available Balance

If you were to subtract the total amount of float from the ledger balance, you would get the collected balance. If there is no float in an account, then the collected and ledger balances will be identical.

Sometimes the bank will refer to this balance as a "collected" balance. While there is a technical distinction between "collected" and "available" balances, it is of little practical importance.

It is important to always read the fine print on any disclosure forms your bank gives you, and to ask questions whenever you are not sure about its policies.

6. DIRECT DEPOSITS

One of the most underutilized services available through banks is that of having money from an employer, the government, a union—almost any organization that owes you money—automatically deposited to your checking or savings account. This service is safe, fast, and convenient, and you should make sure that you inquire about it.

Virtually every bank, savings and loan, and credit union has this service available at no cost to you. Often, your bank will make special benefits, such as free checking, available with it. The main difference between these direct deposit services and other, more familiar, banking services is that direct deposit requires the participation of your employer, union, or other paying body that issues these payments.

What's In It for You?

The direct deposit program was designed by banks in the 1970s to take advantage of the rapidly developing computer banking technology. It has taken almost a decade for the service to begin to be widely adopted, largely because bankers have been very ineffective in explaining the benefits of the system for you, the consumer. There are many benefits to direct deposit:

• There is no waiting in line to deposit your paycheck.

- The paycheck is deposited whether or not you can get to the bank on payday.

- If you earn interest on your checking account, you will earn more, since the direct deposit goes in without float.

- It is safer than a check, since you can't lose a direct deposit "check" or be robbed en route to the bank.

- Once the funds are in your account, they can't be "returned." The employer can't stop payment on the check, and the bank that "originated" the deposit is responsible for paying your bank.

Of course, not having to go to the bank does not mean you have no need for cash. These days, however, access to cash is not the problem it used to be. In addition to using grocery stores to cash your personal check, you can use your automated teller machine card to get cash. Thus, direct deposit of payroll and other regularly occurring payments reduces your need to go to the bank without sacrificing your ability to get the cash you need. This is a wonderful benefit that you should use.

What You Need to Do
All you have to do to take advantage of this system is to sign a form, available from your payroll office. There is no charge for this service. Some employers will also ask you to void a check and attach it to this form. This is designed to make sure that the checking account number it sends to the bank is correct.

In addition to the voided check verification, another account number verification also occurs. Once you sign the authorization form for direct deposit, your employer will inform your bank that a deposit is coming. The employer does this by sending through a "zero dollar" deposit to your account. This special transaction alerts the bank to the arrangement between you and your employer and again verifies the account number.

Be sure to ask your payroll department if the bank it uses offers any special accounts for direct deposit. Often, a bank that processes a company's payroll tape offers free checking to employees who open an account.

Payments from the Government

The federal government and many state governments offer and encourage the use of direct deposit for any regularly scheduled payments to individuals. In fact, the federal government has been one of the most active and aggressive users of bank direct deposit services. Any Social Security office will be happy to tell you whether your payment is eligible for direct deposit and, if you are a federal worker or in the military, your payroll office will do the same.

How Does Direct Deposit Work?

Let's look at a typical company-sponsored direct deposit of payroll program. The methods and steps here are identical to those taken for any other type of direct deposit program.

When a company first sets up a direct deposit program, it works through a bank, usually one close to its payroll processing operation. The bank and the company

sign an agreement that basically says that the bank agrees to process the deposits given to it by the company for its employees, and send those deposits to any bank that offers direct deposit services. The company agrees to make sure the bank has enough money to cover all the deposits it sends. This is important because it illustrates a major difference between a check and a direct deposit to your account.

When you deposit a check in your account, you must wait for it to clear, as we discussed in Chapter 4. This leads to the possibility that it could be returned once it gets to the employer's bank. A direct deposit received by your bank, however, is treated like cash. Therefore, there is no float, and once it is in your account, it is immediately available to you, since it can't be returned. That's why this arrangement is so important to you.

Once the agreement between the company and its bank is signed, the company changes its computer system to create a magnetic tape several days before payday. This tape is then sent to the bank. The bank that receives the tape removes from the tape the deposits that belong to its customers, and then creates a new tape with the accounts that belong to other banks. This tape is sent to an "automated clearinghouse."

The automated clearinghouse reads the bank's tape and puts it together with tapes it receives from other banks, sorts the deposits by bank, and sends your bank a tape with all of the deposits the clearinghouse received for its customers, including yours. Your bank receives the tape the night before payday, so it can credit the deposit to your account and make the funds available to you on payday.

7. AUTOMATED TELLER MACHINES (ATMS)

An increasingly important consideration when you choose a bank is its automated teller machine (ATM) services. These machines have come a long way from the clunkers that, fifteen years ago, simply took deposits and gave cash. Today, they are flexible account servicing machines that can dispense information as well as cash and perform numerous banking services.

Types of ATMs
There are essentially three types of ATMs, differing chiefly in their sophistication. The more sophisticated a machine is, the more useful it is.

First there is the limited service machine called a "cash dispenser." This machine does not take deposits; its functions are limited to cash dispensing.

Second is the full-service ATM, which can take deposits, dispense cash, and accept bill payments.

Third, the latest version of the full-service ATM will talk to you, has a color screen, and can transfer funds among virtually all of your various accounts at the bank. It can even print a statement while you wait.

The Advantages of an ATM
What are the advantages and disadvantages of these machines? First, the major advantages:

Complete flexibility of banking when you want it—not just when the bank is open. These machines are normally available twenty-four hours a day.

Faster transactions. When you go to cash a check, you have to provide ID and stand in line behind people embroiled in complex transactions. An ATM will dispense cash at the touch of a couple of buttons and—because it is designed to handle the more common transactions—is like an express line.

Easier access to your cash. Increasingly, banks are joining "networks" that give you access to machines at other banks, often even in other states. This makes it possible to obtain cash hundreds of miles from home.

Current information about your account balance.

The Disadvantages of an ATM
There are, however, some disadvantages to using ATMs, and you should be aware of these, as well:

Safety. Getting cash at an unattended ATM in the dark of night is not without its risks. The bad guys know that when you're standing at the machine, there is probably cash in your pocket—or soon will be.

Record keeping is more difficult. Since you can get access to your cash without your checkbook, it is more difficult than ever to remember to enter the withdrawal in your check register. Consequently, it is easier than ever to overdraw your account.

Cost. ATM usage can be more expensive than check writing. What used to be promoted by banks as a free service is increasingly becoming a fee-based service.

Machine malfunctions. When God gave man the computer, He evidently also decreed that for every umpteen computer transactions, there would be a certain number of calamities. ATMs sometimes shut down just when you want them most. ATMs have also been known to "eat" offending access cards, leaving their owners angry and cashless on busy weekends or holidays.

Minimizing the Disadvantages
Here's how you can minimize the disadvantages of using an ATM:

Safety
The amount of security a bank can provide at an ATM location is limited. Many banks put ATMs in locked lobbies or kiosks that can be entered only by using a valid ATM card. This is only illusory safety, however, since the lobbies or kiosks are usually visible from the street, and the bad guys can always wait until you come out. The best safety tip regarding your own personal safety is to use simple common sense:

- At night, use well-lit ATMs in places where there are other people around (in many areas of the country, supermarkets have ATMs right in the stores).

- Use drive-up ATMs so you can stay in your car while you make your deposit or withdrawal.

• Always "case" the area around the ATM before approaching it to make sure there are no suspicious-looking strangers in the immediate vicinity.

Record Keeping

ATM users who aren't great record keepers can maintain better control over their accounts with a small amount of up-front organization. The secret is to use two accounts with your card: a checking account and a savings account. The basic outline of the process is this:

1. Ask your company to make the direct deposit of your paycheck to your savings account, or deposit your paycheck yourself at the bank to your savings account.

2. Transfer the amount of money you will need for your monthly bills from the savings account to the checking account. Your bank should be able to put both account numbers on the same ATM card so you can make the transfer right at the ATM.

3. Use your checking account for monthly bills and writing other checks.

4. Make all of your ATM cash withdrawals out of the savings account, not the checking account.

Unlike on a checking account, you can trust the balance the bank gives you on a savings account to be the amount of money available for withdrawal.

In a checking account, the bank can give you your balance as of that day (technically the end of the prior

day), but it has no way of telling what checks might come in that day from other banks. Therefore, if you make withdrawals based on the balance the bank gives you for checking, you could end up withdrawing more than you should and bouncing the next check that comes in. For this privilege, your bank could charge you as much as $25 in fees. The balance in a savings account, on the other hand, is really the amount you have available, since there are no checks to clear.

Another way to protect yourself from overdrawing your account is to apply for your bank's "overdraft protection" line of credit. These lines of credit are called by many different names, but if you ask for "overdraft protection," the banker will know what you mean. With overdraft protection, when you overdraw your account, the bank automatically loans you an amount sufficient to cover the overdraft up to the amount of credit you have previously established.

Cost

Smart shopping is the best way to minimize fees from ATM usage. When you talk to a banker about opening an account, make sure you ask what "network" the bank belongs to. One of the major advantages of ATMs is the flexibility you have in gaining access to your money. Not only is this flexibility measured in the number of hours in the day that you can reach your money, but also in the number of ATM locations throughout the area where you can make cash withdrawals.

Networks appeared in the banking world about ten years ago and were generally limited to a few banks. When banks joined together to make a network, they

were basically saying that customers of Bank A could use the ATM of Bank B to make withdrawals from Bank A's account. Over the years these networks have joined other networks to make nationwide networks. Today your bank is probably a member of one of these national networks. The CIRRUS network, for example, can provide access to ATMs at over 20,000 locations in the U.S. and Canada. Some other national networks are PLUS, MOST, Network Exchange, and Cash Flow.

Access to this wide network of ATMs will usually cost you money. Fees for using network machines are typically between $.75 and $1.50 per transaction. Is this expensive? It depends. It's cheap if, for example, you live in New York and need cash when you're in San Francisco and nobody (big surprise) will cash your personal check. It can also be cheaper than paying the fee to purchase traveler's checks.

It's expensive, however, if you are paying network charges because your local bank does not have branches or ATMs in areas convenient to your workplace or residence. One advantage of dealing with a bank that has many branches is that it will usually provide an account that allows you to use its ATMs for free.

Banks that do charge for network transactions are not necessarily gouging their customers. Bank A has to pay a fee to Bank B every time Bank A's customers use Bank B's machines. Therefore, Bank A may feel justified in charging you for this activity.

Of course, not all banks make such network charges, and this can work to your advantage. Often, smaller banks with few branches realize that a good way to get your business is to offer extremely low-cost checking

accounts, sometimes with interest, and not charge you for network ATM transactions. This way they pay a fee for each transaction you make, but they have a checking account and its average balance that they wouldn't ordinarily get.

If you are in the market for an inexpensive checking account and you like to use ATMs, consider looking at some of the smaller banks, credit unions, or S&Ls in your area. Find out if they belong to a network, and what, if any, charge they make for its use. Combine this with direct deposit of your paycheck and you can get a free checking account and unlimited nationwide ATM access, and will never have to go back to the bank after you've opened the account.

Deposits at ATMs

The sign of a true ATM junkie is trusting not only withdrawals to the machine but deposits as well. You are truly hooked when you trust not only check deposits to the machine, but cash deposits!

You should be aware of a couple of aspects of ATM deposit usage. First, what happens when you enter your deposit in that little slot? Actually, not much. Your envelope falls into a bin where it remains until the machine is "settled." Then the deposit is removed by two tellers (banks like to call this "dual control") under the theory that two are less likely to steal than one. The envelopes are opened, and the deposits are processed by a teller just as if you were standing at a teller window. In practical terms, making a deposit at an ATM is not much more than dropping it in a hole (albeit a very safe hole) for the bank to process later.

This process should indicate why it is important that you include a deposit ticket with your deposit. You should also clearly indicate your account number when you endorse the check.

One aspect of ATM deposits is especially important to you. When a bank "settles" an ATM it means that at that point in time, all of the day's processing is complete, and any deposit made at the machine for the rest of the day is ignored until the next day. This can be tricky because many banks settle their ATM machine before the branch is closed. Therefore, if you need to make a deposit to cover checks you have written, you may have to wait in the teller line to make that deposit if the ATM has already "settled" for the day. If you make a deposit after the settlement time, you delay the processing of your deposit by one full business day.

Computer Malfunctions

There is only so much you can do about computer glitches. It can be helpful to use your ATM during regular banking hours, so if the machine burps, a real live human is available to help. This is not always feasible, of course, so a second-best option is to use an ATM at a bank branch, rather than a stand-alone unit at a gas station or other public location. Then, if the ATM eats your card, you can call the branch first thing in the morning the next day and try to intercept your card before it reaches the shredder.

Getting a replacement ATM card can be a real problem—weeks of waiting at some banks. So, it might be worth finding out in advance what your bank's procedures are when a problem (inevitably) occurs. It might

also be handy to have a back-up ATM card, if your bank will let you have one. If your bank won't, there are probably banks in your area that will.

8. SAVINGS AND INVESTMENTS

Any written, legal document can technically be considered an "instrument." There are a host of financial instruments and accounts offered by banks. The most common are certificates of deposit and savings accounts. Other instruments include treasury bills, stocks, bonds, and commercial paper. Let's take a look at them.

Savings Accounts

Passbooks were the traditional record-keeping device issued for a savings account. The name comes from the small booklet used for the account. The bank enters your balance and any interest earned each time you make a deposit or withdrawal. Today, many older customers still insist on having a passbook as proof of the account's existence. These customers want to physically see each deposit, withdrawal, and interest credit posted on the date it actually occurs. The account holder brings his passbook to the bank whenever a deposit or withdrawal is made. The bank updates the passbook.

Because the process of updating passbooks is so time-consuming, fewer banks are offering passbook accounts. Banks that do, tend to pay lower interest rates on passbook accounts than they pay on regular or statement accounts (e.g., 4.5 percent instead of 5.5 percent) in order to discourage them.

Savings accounts are not the "passé" account that those more sophisticated in alternative financial opportunities may think. Some form of a savings account is the basis of all financial management programs and is the basic building block for financial opportunities. Historically, "thrifts" (mutual savings banks and savings and loans) received most of the savings deposits. Commercial banks traditionally neglected savings accounts because they were considered personal accounts instead of the commercial accounts they so carefully sought. Many savings banks opened in New England in the late seventeenth and eighteenth centuries to encourage thrift and to provide a place for the smaller saver to deposit his savings. Established to fill similar needs, S&Ls accepted deposits from individuals and extended home mortgage credit—something considered by commercial banks to be beneath their dignity.

Since World War II, commercial banks have come to place more emphasis on the personal savings account. They have realized that these accounts represent a valuable source of funds.

Savings accounts are more stable than demand deposits (checking accounts) because the frequency of withdrawals is much less, since no checks are provided with a standard savings account. This works in your favor, as it is the reason banks generally pay higher interest on savings accounts than on checking accounts.

A savings account may be opened as an individual, joint, or fiduciary account held in trust for someone else. Like a checking account, a savings account is opened with forms to be filled out and signature cards to be signed. If it is a joint account, you will also have to de-

cide if the account will be 1) a joint account with rights of survivorship or 2) as tenants-in-common.

Saving gives you the feeling of confidence and the security of knowing that there will be reserves to fall back on in case of need. Saving takes planning, determination, and self-control over your spending habits.

However, if you are like many people, planning, determination, and self-control are often difficult to put into practice. If you are one of these people, look into "forced savings" plans offered by many banks. With these plans, money is automatically deducted from your checking account and transferred to savings.

Savings accounts are an ideal way to put aside your hard-earned money but have it available at any time. There are three types of savings accounts: "regular" or "statement" savings, "money market deposit" accounts, and "time deposit" accounts. These accounts have very different features, so you must decide which one is best for you.

Are you looking for the highest interest rate possible? Or is liquidity (being able to convert your savings readily into cash) what you need first and foremost? Can you meet the minimum balance requirements? Can your money be tied up for a predetermined length of time? Generally speaking, you will receive more interest the longer you are able to leave your money in an account which has the greatest minimum balance.

Statement Savings Accounts

Today's technology has made the passbook obsolete. The regular or statement account has all but replaced the passbook account. A statement savings account has no

length of time requirements, and if there is any minimum balance requirement at all, it is usually very low.

While few banks, if any, have fees associated with savings accounts, be sure to check your bank's policies. Some banks assess a service charge if the balance drops below a specified minimum amount over the statement period. Some banks also require advance notification for large withdrawals or the closing of a savings account. Be sure to get clarification on these two points.

Depending on the bank, monthly or quarterly statements will be mailed to you showing all transactions, deposits, withdrawals, interest credit, and the date that each occurred. Statement savings accounts, like the passbook account, have no fixed maturity date. The difference is that the information appears on a regularly cycled statement and does not take up time-consuming efforts in the branch on the actual date of the activity. Most banks offer access to automated teller machines with your statement savings account. One advantage of a passbook or statement savings account is that for the small saver, there is less likely to be fees on these accounts (unless your balance falls below $50 to $100, depending on the bank), unlike the money market deposit account which we'll discuss later. Usually the trade-off of high interest rates for no fees is more profitable for the smaller account. Some banks do not pay any interest below minimum amount.

Money Market Deposit Accounts

Once having set some money aside in a savings account, you may want to open a money market deposit account (MMDA). This is a savings account that has limited

check writing capabilities as well as unlimited deposit and withdrawal features. The limitation on the check writing is that you can only write three checks per month, as mandated by the federal government.

Bank advertising will usually say you can "write" three checks per month. There is a technicality involving this limit that can cost you money. Technically, the limit mandated by the Feds is on the number of checks *paid* out of the account each month, not how many checks you *write*. If you write three checks each month and everyone who gets your check immediately cashes or deposits it, there will usually not be a problem. But, if one of them delays depositing the check, you could find yourself in violation, because that check will not clear until the next month's statement, when four checks will clear instead of the three allowed. When this happens, your bank will probably apply a service charge to your MMDA account.

Normally, there is a minimum balance imposed by the bank—not the federal government—of $1000 to $2500 to open a money market deposit account. Some banks pay no interest and/or impose fees on money market deposit accounts if the balance falls below the minimum amount.

Banks determine their own rates of interest based on their particular formulas. These rates will rise and fall depending on the overall national economy. Banks can pay any rate of interest they want, so shop for the best deal you can get. If your balance falls below the minimum balance, most banks will drop the interest rate to a minimum rate (usually 5.5 percent). Sometimes a service charge may also be added to the account.

All banks have the legal right to request advance notice of large withdrawals or the closing of savings and money market deposit accounts. Few banks impose this policy under normal circumstances, but it serves as a safety for the bank if it has to impose the policy due to financial constraints.

Time Deposit Accounts

As time goes on and your system of savings and earnings increases, you may wish to consider opening a "time deposit" account. Many people continue to maintain regular savings accounts and/or money market deposit accounts for liquidity purposes and open a time deposit account for greater interest earnings.

A time deposit account, also known as a "certificate of deposit" (CD), is an account whereby you contract with the bank to leave a certain amount of money in the bank for a predetermined period of time (anywhere from seven days to many years). There is a specified term with a fixed maturity date. There are rarely any fees on these accounts. Since deregulation, many banks offer time deposit accounts without early withdrawal penalties, but check the fine print to be sure. Some banks, too, will send you interest checks instead of paying interest back into the time deposit account. You will earn more if the interest is paid directly back into the time deposit account rather than being sent to you or deposited into some other account.

Remember to read all the fine print when you buy. Compare minimum purchase amounts, early withdrawal penalities, and above all, the annual percentage rate disclosure. If you need some of the money before the CD

matures, you may be able to cash it in with no early withdrawal penalty. So shop carefully before you buy.

There is no guarantee, however, that you will be able to buy another CD with the same rate if you want to reinvest the balance of the funds. Therefore, don't just buy one CD. For, say $5000, buy five $1000 CDs. That way if you néed a little cash, you can cash one in without losing the interest rate on the other four. This assumes, of course, that the new rate would be lower. If rates have gone up and you have no withdrawal penalty, the best financial strategy would be for you to cash them all in and buy at the higher rate.

The negotiable certificate of deposit, as we know the account today, was first introduced in 1961. A wide variety of terms and conditions, including accounts with fixed-ceiling interest rates and variable rates, are available and can be "negotiated" by the customer. Typically, the minimum deposits for each category are stated with the terms available for CDs. The following chart shows the typical maturity periods available for CDs. Normally, the longer the period, the higher the interest rate.

Typical CD Maturity Periods

7 to 89 days	2 to 2 1/2 years
90 days to 1 year	30 to 41 months
91 days	2 1/2 to 4 years
6 months	4 to 6 years
12 months	6 to 8 years
1 to 2 years	8 years+

How to Save Money

How do you begin to save money, especially when there seems barely enough to pay the monthly bills? First, set a goal for yourself, whether it is a new stereo system, a stove, a car, or a down payment for a house. Make reminders for yourself—for example, a picture of the goal or written note on your refrigerator—to guard against the temptation to buy extra or unnecessary items.

Consider your savings as an additional expense, and make it a regular part of your bill-paying sessions. You will now be paying towards your goal, thus paying yourself for your efforts. The key is to begin to save as soon as possible and then to save on a regular basis.

Small savings deposits on a regular basis add up faster than you might think. Another guide that many financial managers use is that 10 percent of one's annual earnings should be saved. One way to do this, if willpower is not working, is to have your bank set up an automatic savings plan whereby the bank automatically withdraws a certain amount from your checking account and places it in your savings account. This is a forced way to save that has grown in popularity as many people find it very convenient.

Depending on your finances and your stage in life, you must ultimately decide which type or combination of savings account(s) is best for you. If you are just starting out in your first job, you should probably consider opening a regular or statement savings account. As your assets grow, you may wish to open a money market deposit account or certificate of deposit as a way to diversify your savings and earn more interest. There are other financial instruments that usually have more risk at-

tached to them, but may increase your investment power if funds are invested wisely.

Treasury Bills

Most banks sell treasury bills, which are essentially an I.O.U. from the government. The federal government issues these "T-bills" for periods of 90, 180, and 360 days, with $10,000 being the least amount that can be invested. There are also treasury notes, which have maturity periods of one to ten years, and treasury bonds, whose maturity periods are over ten years.

Banks usually charge a fee for selling these, unless you have substantial deposits with the bank. You may also purchase treasury bills directly from a Federal Reserve bank or through the mail, usually without being charged a fee.

"T-bills" are known as a discounted investment because your earnings are calculated directly into the purchase price. At a 10 percent rate for a 360-day T-bill worth $10,000, your actual investment would be $9000. At the end of the period, the government would send you a check for $10,000. If you have to sell the T-bill before the period is up, no penalty is imposed. The amount you will receive will depend on market conditions at the time of the sale.

Stocks and Bonds

Stocks may be sold by some banks through their discount brokerage division. No advice is offered by a discount broker, but all transactions (the buying and selling of stocks) can be handled at a lower rate than that of a full-service broker.

Many banks also sell bonds, but usually through their trust divisions. Bonds are issued by large corporations, municipalities, and other government entities to raise funds, often for a specific project (e.g., highways, civic centers, or a corporate need). The issuer promises to repay the specified debt by a certain period of time. Bonds are less liquid than stocks and usually require at least $10,000 as a minimum investment.

Commercial Paper

Few banks sell commercial paper to individuals because of the amount of investment involved (upwards of $30,000). Commercial paper is a corporate I.O.U. for a term of less than one year. It is an unsecured method corporations use to borrow funds. It is a higher risk than other investments and does not carry deposit insurance.

Retirement Accounts

Retirement accounts are other products offered by banks for saving. These became popular, both as a way to save for the retirement years and as a federal income tax break. Introduced in 1974, the Employee Retirement Income Security Act (ERISA) was established to allow qualified individuals to establish their own tax-sheltered plans with banks and other financial intermediaries.

Individual Retirement and Keogh Accounts

Individual retirement accounts (IRAs) are time-deposit accounts where working individuals can deposit up to $2000 each year. If a spouse is unemployed, the working spouse can contribute $2250 each year. The interest is tax exempt until the money is withdrawn.

When the plans were first introduced in 1974, up to $2000 (or $2250 if one spouse is unemployed) was considered a federal income tax adjustment. This was an attractive incentive for individuals and couples to save for their retirement. Since the recent tax law changes in 1986, one's income level and participation in his employer's retirement or 401(k) plan are the qualifying criteria for receiving a tax adjustment. Still, to be able to save every year, tax free, is an incentive to many.

Those in business for themselves are eligible to open a Keogh account for their retirement. Keoghs are similar to IRAs, except a higher amount may be contributed each year—up to 15 percent of one's annual salary or $30,000 per year, whichever amount is higher. This is attractive for those who are self-employed, as it presents a savings opportunity for retirement when no corporate pension plans are available.

The minimum age (for both IRAs and Keoghs) when funds *may* be withdrawn without a penalty is fifty-nine and one half. At age seventy and one half, withdrawals *must* be made and a payout plan established.

Once withdrawals are made, the money becomes taxable income. The penalties are quite stiff should you need to withdraw funds before age fifty-nine and one half. Check carefully the terms and agreements of the IRA or Keogh plan so you know just what to expect from this type of retirement account.

To open either a Keogh or an IRA, a written contract is drawn up, very similar to a regular time deposit account. You may also have the same choices for the length of term for this account, fixed or variable interest rate, and opening deposit amount.

Once the account reaches maturity, it may "roll over" automatically or be subject to you coming into the bank and renewing the contract with either the same or different terms and conditions. Due to changing IRS rules on these accounts, it is best to check with an accountant concerning your investment decisions.

9. CREDIT: THE INS AND OUTS

Getting a loan or getting credit is not necessarily a difficult procedure. You must, however, understand the principles behind obtaining credit and the rating system used by banks and finance companies to determine if you as a customer are credit worthy.

When you take out a loan, you are, in effect, renting someone else's money. How do you go about the process of getting a loan and what are some of the factors which must be considered?

Banks Want to Lend Money

First and foremost, remember that banks are in business to make loans. Loans provide upwards of 60-70 percent of a bank's total revenue—by far the largest source of its income—so they want to make them. The three main objectives of a bank in making a loan are:

- *Liquidity*. Banks must maintain their ability to provide for the loan demands of long-established customers in good standing.

- *Safety*. Banks try to eliminate all risks associated with granting loans.There is much truth to the joke that bankers only make loans to people who don't need them.

- *Income.* The income from loans will be used to support the expenses and growth of the institution.

HOW A BANKER LOOKS AT YOU

Your banker or credit officer will look at your ability and willingness to pay back a loan within a certain length of time. To make a fair evaluation, the officer uses the "five Cs of credit": capacity, character, collateral, capital, and credit history. The lender will want to know all he can about you, your habits, and your finances. It frequently helps if you are a current customer of the bank where you are requesting a loan, but if you are in good standing financially, you should have little trouble in obtaining credit from other banks, as well.

Capacity

Your ability—or "capacity"—to repay a loan is of particular importance to a banker. He will question you about personal financial information, including your wage earnings, any other income you may have and the expenses for which you are responsible.

Character

Assessing character is a judgment call on the part of the banker, but it is one he must try to make. Signs of personal and financial stability are critical factors in making an honest appraisal. The length of time you have lived at your current address, whether you have life insurance or own your home are all helpful in making this evaluation. The length of time you have lived in the same residence or worked at the same company shows stability and helps when references are requested.

Collateral

If you were to receive a loan, the bank would want to be protected in case—for any reason—you defaulted on that loan and did not repay it. This is where "collateral" and "capital" play an important part. You need to understand that the bank's determination to get collateral may have nóthing at all to do with its regard for you as an individual. Your situation could radically change in the future—for health, economic, or other reasons—and the bank has to protect itself.

Usually creditors will want to know the reason for the loan and will also want some tangible item as a safety cushion in case you do not repay it. So, the loan is secured by collateral—sort of a back-up system to the loan. If you were to get a new car loan, for example, the collateral would typically be the car itself. If you got a mortgage, you would use the house as collateral.

The lender will want to know about your savings, investments, property, and any other income sources that might be available to repay the debt. This is capital. Capital can also be used as collateral on a loan.

Credit History

Your history of using credit will help the lender decide if you are a good credit risk for the bank. If you have had outstanding loans in the past that have been paid off regularly and on time, your credit history will be a positive force in the overall credit evaluation.

How do you establish credit? When first starting out, young people have a very difficult time showing proof that they are credit worthy. A typical complaint is that you must have credit to get credit.

Those who have had school loans are usually a step ahead in lining up a credit history, and thus have an easier time getting their next loan. Those who have never had any debt must rely on their earnings, job, and any other financial assets that may be used to satisfy the lender's qualifications.

The main reason lenders look at credit history is that it shows how reliable you have been in paying back your borrowed funds. If you have no credit history you must build one.

Building Your Personal Credit History

A first step in building a credit history is to establish checking and savings accounts. These can be used as a source of positive information for the lender when the accounts are shown to be well managed.

When you do have a checking account, try to avoid bouncing checks. That may be taken as a sign that you are not willing to pay your debts and your ability to manage your finances is poor.

Your first loan might be for an item where you borrow against your savings account. The interest on the loan would be slightly offset by the interest you receive on your savings account, therefore reducing the cost of the loan. You could also borrow against an existing asset, such as a car, using it as collateral to secure the loan.

Cosigners

A relative or friend might be willing to cosign a loan application with you if you cannot get credit on your own. The cosigner would share the responsibility with you, and would have to pay back the loan if you did not.

Open Credit Card Accounts

Opening one or two credit card accounts is a useful way to establish credit. Be careful not to open too many accounts, though, as lenders are cautious if too much credit is available.

This can be done at local department stores or gas stations, but you should be aware that many local department stores keep surprisingly sloppy records and could damage your credit history unfairly through sheer ineptitude. It is safer to rely on major credit cards—VISA, MasterCard, Sears, etc.—to do your local shopping and to establish your credit history.

Discrimination

In the past, discrimination has existed for certain groups of people: women, young adults, the elderly, and minorities. To deal with this problem, the "Equal Credit Opportunity Act" was enacted a number of years ago. It states that race, color, age, religion, sex, marital status, and other factors may not be used to discriminate against someone when determining the level of credit risk. This law has helped alleviate the bias.

Redlining—the act of accepting deposits from deteriorating neighborhoods but not granting loans in those areas because the perceived risk is too great—is another bias that some communities have felt, particularly in our inner cities. Federal bank examinations now include assessments of the credit level extended in all communities where a bank does business, so as to alleviate this particular problem.

But let's be honest here. Discrimination in America is a fact of life and cannot be completely eliminated by

government edict. The situation is dramatically better than it used to be, but bias still exists. The good news is that, should you have trouble with one bank, you can almost certainly find another in your community that will treat you fairly.

Don't accept discriminatory treatment from your bank. If you have any doubts as to your rights, see a lawyer or obtain advice from your local government.

People get in trouble when credit is overused, not when credit is put to use in a well-managed way. The standard rule of borrowing is to borrow only the amount you need for a much-needed item.

10. COMMON TYPES OF LOANS

Before you begin looking for the right loan, you must understand the elements of a loan, namely the interest cost you will pay, which is based on the principal (the amount borrowed), the term (the length of time you take to repay the loan), and the rate of interest. The finance charge is the total payment you owe for borrowing the money and includes the interest charge, possible service charges, and credit insurance costs.

Interest Rates and APR

Interest rates must be stated in annual percentage rate (APR) terms, according to the federal Truth in Lending law. The APR makes it easier for you to understand the true cost of the loan on a yearly basis because it factors in any fees or "points" paid for the loan. For this reason, just as the effective annual yield is the most accurate measure of the interest you earn on a deposit account, the APR is the most accurate measure of the loan's real cost. For your protection, the APR must be disclosed in writing on all agreements you are reviewing. This is true for all types of charge cards, lines of credit, loans, and mortgages. Interest rates are volatile, and the terms of loans change at banks depending on such factors as the demand for loans, the competition, and the flow of money in the economy.

To cite an example, if $100 is the principal and the APR is 12 percent, the finance charge is $12. You would be able to borrow $100 and, at the end of the year, pay back the total (including finance charges) for $112. You would have had use of the $100 for the entire year.

If, on the other hand, you had to pay back the $112 in 12 equal installments, you would have paid $9.33 each month. Not only would you not have had use of the entire $100, but you would effectively be paying an annual rate (APR) of 21.5 percent. It is very helpful to make written comparisons of different loan options, especially where the rate of interest and term of the loan will be variables. Remember, though, that the APR is the true cost of the loan, no matter what a banker may advertise or say to you in a conversation. So, when comparing loan terms, always pay closest attention to the APR.

HOME MORTGAGES

Home mortgages have been the mainstay of savings banks and S&Ls. Now commercial banks and credit unions are finding an active mortgage market for their customers, too.

Traditionally, the fixed-rate thirty-year mortgage was the only mortgage available. Now there is quite an assortment of mortgages, including those with fifteen-year terms and adjustable rates. The adjustable-rate mortgages (ARMs) have become almost as popular as the fixed-rate mortgage, due to high interest rates in the early 1980s. The security of knowing what the interest rate will be on a fixed-rate mortgage and, consequently, what your monthly payments will be usually makes the

conventional mortgage more expensive than the new ARM introduced in the late seventies.

The key to evaluating a mortgage is the APR. The annual percentage rate is usually higher than the percentage rate quoted in the newspaper or in a brochure because the points are included in the APR.

Points

A new addition to the mortgage field during the 1970s was "points"—up-front charges imposed by the lender and paid in cash at the "closing" (the time the loan is signed). Points are really percentages. One point equals one percent of the loan principal. So, if you want a $100,000 mortgage, a single point will cost you an extra $1000 in cash at the time the mortgage is signed. In some markets two, three, or even four points are customarily charged on a mortgage.

The points allow the bank to front load the loan—to get more of its profit from the loan up front instead of waiting for the term to be completed. Often, the more points (and the more cash) paid in the beginning, the lower the percentage rate on the note. If you do not have enough cash for the points, you can often work with your lender to plan a way to fund them.

The combination of the points and interest rate equal the APR, and this should be your guide when comparing mortgages. Remember, though, that when comparing adjustable-rate mortgages and their APRs, the APR is accurate only for the initial period. As soon as the interest rate changes, the APR will change, too.

There is a great deal of variance between many banks concerning the number of points on a loan, the actual

interest rate, and the term of the loan. Many mortgages are now available as a fifteen-year mortgage. Most are still paid in monthly charges, but a few banks have begun offering mortgages that are paid twice a month.

Adjustable-Rate Mortgages (ARMs)

The adjustable-rate mortgage (ARM) has no fixed rate. As the name implies, the rate is subject to change. Typically, this will be a once a year adjustment. There is usually a set margin (in percentage points) in which the rate can rise and fall. This is based on some financial index such as the prime rate.

The initial rate is usually lower than with a conventional fixed-rate mortgage, so the risk of the loan's interest rate fluctuating up is on the borrower. The risk lies in the fact that you do not know when interest rates will rise. Limits on the interest rate rising are critical to your managing a budget. When interest rates are high, ARMs are more affordable and more popular to a borrower. When interest rates are low, a fixed-rate mortgage is more popular, as borrowers want to lock in a good rate for a long period of time.

When evaluating ARMs, check carefully to see what the interest rate caps are on rising rates. Since the Competitive Equality Banking Act of 1987, all ARMs must have a top rate beyond which interest rates cannot go. The federal government does not set limits on how high the ceiling can rise, leaving the states to set usury caps.

Banks, for their part, usually set annual caps on the amount an ARM can rise each year. It may be wise to forgo an ARM with a low interest rate for one that has lower caps, unless you are sure you will not own that

property for the length of the mortgage. The annual cap is what keeps your payment in check. The lower the cap, the lower the payment.

When comparing ARMs, ask what the maximum lifetime rate is. This is the ARM's lifetime cap added to its first-year interest rate. Then figure out what your monthly payments will be, with the help of a banker or by consulting a loan payments handbook, when the loan is at its peak rate. This should help you determine if the higher payment in the future is realistic and affordable. Then find the best fixed-rate mortgage and calculate that monthly payment. If the fixed-rate mortgage payment is only slightly higher than the first-year rate of an ARM, it is probably wiser to choose the fixed-rate mortgage.

While ARM rates typically change yearly, on some ARMs the rate changes monthly but your payment only changes once a year. If interest rates go up during the year, more and more of each payment goes to interest rather than principal. If rates go up enough, you could end up accruing more interest than you are paying in your monthly payment. Under this type of ARM, your excess interest is added to the loan balance. This is sometimes referred to as "negative amortization." Of course, if rates go down, more of your payment goes to principal but, in general, be very careful of getting involved with this kind of mortage.

Some ARMs have the capability of being converted from an adjustable to a fixed rate. Usually these ARMs have extra point charges and fees. The initial note rate is competitive with other non-convertible ARMs, but when you convert, the rate will be a little higher than that of a fixed-rate mortgage at the time of conversion.

Information About Mortgage Rates

To get public information about mortgage rates in your area, look in your local paper or contact HSH Associates, the nation's largest publisher of mortgage information. They also offer a home buyer's mortgage kit, which includes a loan payment table and histories of the most popular mortgage indexes. The kit and two weekly rate reports cost $18. Over 2000 lenders are surveyed in several metropolitan areas. HSH Associates can be reached toll free at 1-800-UPDATES. Their address is:

HSH Associates
10 Mead Avenue
Riverdale, NJ 07457

Mortgage Indexes

The rate at which an ARM's interest rate can change is tied to the financial index chosen by the bank. It may be monthly or more or less frequent. It is wise to evaluate which index your bank uses, because you may have to decide whether an ARM with a two-point cap using a less volatile index is preferable to an ARM with a one-point cap using a more volatile index.

Each time the rate is adjusted, the new rate is determined by adding a set number of percentage points to the index. The number of percentage points that can be affixed per year is stated in the original loan agreement. The most common index used is the one-year treasury security rate, but some banks use the Federal Home Loan Bank Board's (FHLBB) cost of funds index, prime rate, the treasury rate, or the National Mortgage Contract Interest Rate Index.

Knowing what index will be used to adjust your mortgage rate is as important as knowing what the annual cap is because of the degree of sensitivity different indexes have to economic factors such as inflation. The more volatile the index, the greater the chance of the annual adjustments rising. The FHLBB cost of funds index is less volatile than the prime rate or one-year treasury rate, because it is based on the cost of savings deposits at banks and S&Ls in the eleventh district, which includes California, Nevada, and Arizona. It is a monthly index.

Mortgage Insurance and Other Add-ons

Once you have locked yourself into that mortgage payment, you will have to decide if mortgage insurance is necessary. Usually, if your down payment is at least 10 percent of the purchase price, there will be no bank requirement to purchase insurance as a safety to the bank in case you default on your payment.

Another type of mortgage insurance provides for the continued payments on your home in the event that something happens to your spouse. You will also have to decide if you wish your mortgage payment to include additional funds for an escrow account to pay any annual insurance premiums and real estate taxes. Do not be surprised to learn that, due to increased real estate taxes in your area, your mortgage payment might increase every year.

Home Equity Loans

Since changes in the tax laws have eliminated interest deductions from personal credit and installment loans, borrowers are beginning to use home equity loans to

purchase automobiles, consolidate debt, and even finance vacations and investments.

The rates on home equity loans are lower than on charge cards and personal loans. There may, in fact, be as much as a six- or seven-percentage point difference between a personal and an equity loan. Most credit cards and personal loans are unsecured. Equity loans are secured with your home and use the market value of your home (less any outstanding mortgage) as collateral.

Equity loans include second mortgages in which you would receive a lump sum loan amount, home improvement loans, and revolving lines of credit. The lines of credit only charge interest when all or part of the principal is borrowed. Equity loans may be fixed- or variable-rate loans, depending on the bank. If you must use a home equity loan, a fixed-rate second mortgage is the best because variable rates on these loans do not have the built-in caps that adjustable-rate mortgages have. If there is a cap, it is usually quite high, eighteen to twenty-one percentage points, not dissimilar from a credit card. Revolving credit lines are variable rate loans that usually have a very attractive initial rate for three to six months.

You should always approach any loan using your home as collateral with considerable caution. That $20,000 dream trip around the world may be the experience of a lifetime, but is it worth risking your home?

AUTOMOBILE LOANS

Fixed-rate loans, also known as installment loans, are still the most common car loans. However, adjustable-rate car loans are becoming more common. Some banks

are even offering home-equity car loans instead of an actual automobile loan. Credit unions frequently offer the best deal on a car loan, but that will depend on the availability of credit unions and competition among lending institutions in your area.

Again, be sure to check the annual percentage rate (APR) for finding the best rate. Frequently, banks add on new fees such as filing or processing fees, document or loan fees, points, or title fees which will be factored into the APR.

Adjustable-rate automobile loans usually have an initial interest rate that is not much lower than that of a fixed rate. When the APR is reviewed, the overall rate is usually as high as the fixed rate. Most banks do not have any caps on these loans, so beware. Like the home equity loan, the variable-rate lifetime caps, if they do exist, are as high as many credit cards.

The term of an automobile loan is also a subject you should consider. Generally, you can get a longer term on a new car than on a used one, and on a more expensive new car than on a less expensive new car. Two-year (twenty-four-month) loans used to be the maximum, but forty-eight-month loans are now common, and sixty-month loans are seen more and more often. These extended loans can seem quite attractive, but you should always be cautious in making any loan.

The problem with long-term automobile loans is that you may not want to keep your car for four or five years. Depending on the car you buy and your driving habits, it might not last that long, either. With a forty-eight-or-sixty-month loan, you will probably have no real equity in the car until it is three or four years old—if then. If

you are forced to sell or trade your car after two or three years, you may actually have to come up with cash (on top of the resale value of the car) to pay off the loan. That can be a pretty grisly surprise if you are unexpectedly out of a job or facing other financial difficulties.

OTHER TYPES OF LOANS

There are other types of loans that are similar to the ones mentioned above. Boat loans are quite similar in structure to a car loan. Personal loans can have fixed or variable rates and can be secured or unsecured, and lines of credit are not charged to you until you actually access the line, using the principal for some purpose. Lines of credit may be reused again and again. Once the line gets paid down, it can be accessed again for some other purpose. Lines of credit may also have fixed or variable interest rates and are used primarily as a cash advance to make purchases.

Credit can be an effective financial management tool. If utilized properly and with the proper respect, credit will afford you the opportunity to enjoy certain benefits now and pay for them later. But there is a price for using this privilege, and that is the cost of the finance charge added onto the purchase price. You must be careful to always keep your payments up to date and discuss any unforeseen problems with your lender, so he knows you are not just being negligent. The amount of credit you carry will depend on your stage in life, income level, and many other factors. Borrow only when you are sure that you can handle the debt, the purpose is worthwhile, and now is the best time.

11. WHAT ELSE DO BANKS OFFER?

Many of the larger banks offer estate planning services, from administering trusts and guardianships and settling estates, to financial planning and counseling.

Estate or Trust Services

A trust is a relationship whereby one party holds property belonging to another, with some particular benefit in mind to the owner. A "trustee" assumes the responsibilities of holding the property and administering the assets for the benefit of the "beneficiary." A trustee can be a bank, an individual, or a corporation. A bank offering trust services must act in the best interest of the client serving as the "fiduciary" for the account.

Estate or trust services include the settling of an estate. Banks may assist in the administration and distribution of an estate if proper arrangements have been made ahead of time for the bank to do so. There are also different trust funds administered by banks:

- Testamentary trusts are created by the decedent's will. The bank's duties include managing the assets and paying income to the named beneficiaries.
- Living trusts are created by individuals who have transferred property to the bank for management.
- Trust departments also offer conservatorship or

guardianship services. These are established by a court order, usually for the benefit of a minor.

- Trust departments also provide "safekeeping" of whatever property a customer requests. Usually this is in the form of stocks, bonds, and other assets.
- "Custody" includes safekeeping along with the collection of income from the assets and generally managing the account.
- Individual Retirement Plans and Keough accounts are also available through the trust department.
- Financial planning and counseling are other services performed by Trust.

There are, of course, fees for all the services offered. In return, trust departments offer the convenience of having all of one's investments managed under one roof, such as accessibility to funds through the bank, expertise in financial management, full service for vault usage, paying bills, writing wills, and filing tax returns.

International Services
Large regional and money center banks have International Divisions where a traveler's letters of credit can be arranged. This is a service planned ahead of time for the sophisticated traveler who expects to make sizable purchases abroad and needs confirmation of the payment of funds up to a certain limit.

Normally, international divisions perform minimal tasks for consumers, such as foreign currency exchange and traveler's checks. International Divisions also can arrange letters of introduction to establish their customers' as creditworthy individuals with foreign banks.

Safe Deposit Boxes

Almost all banks offer safe deposit boxes as rental units for the safekeeping of documents, silver, jewelry, and whatever else is considered irreplaceable. A customer must fill out a signature card when obtaining a safe deposit box. Then, each time a deposit or withdrawal of some item is made into the box, the customer must sign in and out. The use of a safe deposit box is usually done in private and in such a way that no one else will handle or see the items in the box unless the customer is there to direct them to do so.

12. IF SOMETHING GOES WRONG AT YOUR BANK...

What are your legal rights if something goes wrong at your bank, be it with a loan, credit card, or an ATM? Whom can you contact, and what can be done?

Talk to the Branch Manager

It seems elementary, but your first line of defense should be the manager or loan officer at your branch. If your complaint has merit, he should be willing to set matters right. If so, your problem is solved. If not, read on....

Contact Your State's Attorney General

If you are dissatisfied with the treatment you get from a bank, credit bureau, loan company, collection agency, or credit card company—and they won't help—contact your city and/or state attorney general's office. These offices are there to act as watchdogs for your rights.

Usually, state laws are strict in upholding the rights of consumers, and quick action should follow. However, if you feel the response at the local and state level is inadequate, there are several federal agencies you can turn to. If the problem is with a bank, you can contact whichever of the following agencies is appropriate.

• For national banks (or those with N.A. after their name) write to:

The Comptroller of the Currency
Consumer Affairs Division
Washington, DC 20219

• For banks that are state chartered and members of the Federal Reserve System, contact:
Board of Governors
The Federal Reserve System
Director
Division of Consumer Affairs
Washington, DC 20551

• For state-chartered banks that are insured by the Federal Deposit Insurance Corporation (FDIC), but which are not a member of the Federal Reserve System, contact:
Federal Deposit Insurance Corporation
Office of Bank Customer Affairs
Washington, DC 20429

• For federally chartered or insured savings and loans, write to:
Federal Home Loan Bank Board
Washington, DC 20552

• For credit unions that are federally chartered:
Federal Credit Union Administration
Division of Consumer Affairs
Washington, DC 20456

• If any other finance companies or credit card companies are involved, contact the headquarters of the Federal Trade Commission or one of their regional offices:

Federal Trade Commission
Washington, DC 20580

Atlanta Regional Office
1718 Peachtree Street, N.W.
Atlanta, Georgia 30309

Boston Regional Office
1301 Analex Building
Suite 1000, 150 Causeway
Boston, Massachusetts 02114

Cleveland Regional Office
Suite 500, 118 St. Clair
Cleveland, Ohio 44114

Chicago Regional Office
Suite 1437
The Mall Building
55 East Monroe Street
Chicago, Illinois 60603

Dallas Regional Office
2001 Bryan Street
Suite 2665
Dallas, Texas 75201

Denver Regional Office
Suite 2900
1405 Curtis Street
Denver, Colorado 80202

Los Angeles Regional Office
11000 Wilshire Boulevard
Room 13209
Los Angeles, California 90024

New York Regional Office
22nd Floor, Federal Building
26 Federal Plaza
New York, New York 10007

San Francisco Regional Office
450 Golden Gate Avenue
San Francisco,
California 94102

Seattle Regional Office
28th Floor,
Federal Building
Box 36005
915 Second Avenue
Seattle, Washington 98174

INDEX